EXPLORING THE WORLD

Adapted from J. Man's *Exploration and Discovery*

JULIE BROWN
ROBERT BROWN

Gareth Stevens Children's Books
MILWAUKEE

For a free color catalog describing Gareth Stevens' list of high-quality children's books, call 1-800-341-3569 (USA) or 1-800-461-9120 (Canada).

Library of Congress Cataloging-in-Publication Data
Brown, Julie, 1962-
    Exploring the world / by Julie Brown, Robert Brown, and John Man.
       p. cm. — (My first reference library)
    Summary: A survey of exploration and discovery from the accomplishments
of ancient explorers to the present-day excursions into space, underwater, and
beneath the earth.
    ISBN 0-8368-0032-X
    1. Discoveries (in geography)—Juvenile literature. [1. Discoveries (in
geography) 2. Explorers.] I. Brown, Robert, 1961- . II. Man, John. III. Title. IV. Series.
G175.B73   1989
910.9—dc20   89-11285

North American edition first published in 1990 by
Gareth Stevens Children's Books
RiverCenter Building, Suite 201
1555 North RiverCenter Drive
Milwaukee, Wisconsin 53212, USA

Photographic credits: Bryan and Cherry Alexander, 25 (bottom); The Bodleian Library, 24; Christian Bonington, 59 (top); Bridgeman Art Library, 21 (top); John Cleare/Mountain Camera, 9, 13 (top), 32-33, 49 (left), 51, 54 (right), 55 (center); ET Archive, 22, 23, 25 (top left and right), 50 (right); Derek Fordham/Arctic Camera, 57; Frank Spooner Pictures, 59 (center); Giraudon, 27; Susan Griggs/Leon Schadeberg, 6, /Victor Englebert, 41 (top), /Robert Azzi, 46, /Anthony Howarth, 47 (top); Sonia Halliday, 6 (bottom); Michael Holford, 14 (left), 18 (right), 35 (top); Hulton Picture Company, 21 (bottom), 30, 37 (bottom), 45 (bottom); Hutchinson Library, 31 (top), 41 (bottom), 43; MacDonald/Aldus Archive, 39, 42, 45 (top); Magnum, 32; Mansell Collection, 33, 40, 50 (left); Mary Evans Picture Library, 53 (bottom), 54 (left); Marion and Tony Morrison, 34, 35 (bottom), 36, 38; National Maritime Museum, 14 (right); Oxford Scientific Films, 13 (bottom), 19, 31 (bottom); Photo Library of Australia, 49 (top); Popperfoto, 15 (top), 47 (bottom); Rapho, 5; Robert Harding Picture Library, 17, /George Douglass Brewerton: *Crossing the Rocky Mountains*, in the collection of the Corcoran Gallery of Art, Gift of William Wilson Corcoran, 29, /Schloss Tegel, East Berlin, 37 (top), 44, 53 (top); Ronan Picture Library, 18 (left); Science Photo Library, 58; Charles Swithinbank, 55 (top); Viking Museum, Oslo, 10; Werner Forman Archive, 15 (bottom)

Maps by Lovell Johns Ltd.
Illustrated by Nick Shewring (Garden Studios) and Eugene Fleury

Cover illustration © 1990 Kurt Meinke: Two mountain climbers risk the hazards of exploring a glacier. One explorer has safely crossed over a crevasse. The second climber leaps for his life as the fragile snow bridge collapses.

Series editors: Neil Champion and Rita Reitci
Research editor: Scott Enk
Educational consultant: Dr. Alistair Ross
Design: Groom and Pickerill
Cover design: Kate Kriege
Picture research: Ann Usborne

Printed in the United States of America

1 2 3 4 5 6 7 8 9 96 95 94 93 92 91 90

Contents

1: REASONS TO EXPLORE

The Earliest Explorers

This map shows how early ▶ people spread across the Earth from 100,000 to 10,000 years ago.

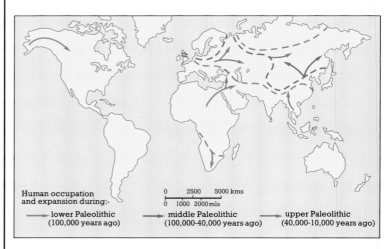

Human occupation and expansion during:-

→ lower Paleolithic (100,000 years ago)

→ middle Paleolithic (100,000-40,000 years ago)

→ upper Paleolithic (40,000-10,000 years ago)

▲ A group of Stone Age people, near the end of the last ice age, around 11,000 years ago.

What Is Exploration?

Over the past 500,000 years, humans migrated from the tropics to cooler climates. By the end of the last ice age, 11,000 years ago, people had spread to every continent except Antarctica. These early humans moved around, looking for better places to live. Explorers are different. They explore to find places to trade, to steal, to learn, to become famous, to settle, or to spread religion. But all explorers have one thing in common. They want to bring or send knowledge of unknown places back to their homelands.

Expanding Nations

Explorers usually came from wealthy, growing nations. Often, explorers were traders who wanted valuable metals, spices, or gems. But some were people interested only in what was beyond the horizon, or scholars who wanted to know more about other peoples, places, and ideas. Most of these explorers experienced great risk and hardship on their journeys.

▲ These paintings of bison are on the walls of caves in Lascaux, France. The pictures are about 30,000 years old, made by people known as Cro-Magnons.

The people below lived for thousands of years before they were "discovered" by European explorers. ▼

New Zealand Maori

Amazonian Indian

Australian Aboriginal

Inuit (Eskimo)

North American Indian

2: THE ANCIENT WORLD

The Birth of Exploration

Mediterranean shores were once clean like this. ▼

The Mediterranean Sea is 2,500 miles (4,000 km) long. It has warm, calm waters and many safe harbors. For hundreds of years, no one living there knew what lay beyond its shores.

Navigation

Early sailors steered by wind direction, stars, currents, and

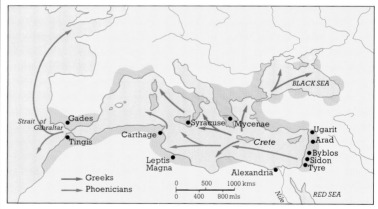

BLACK SEA

Strait of Gibraltar · Gades · Syracuse · Mycenae · Ugarit · Arad
· Tingis · Carthage · Crete · Byblos · Sidon · Tyre
Leptis Magna · Alexandria
→ Greeks
→ Phoenicians
RED SEA
Nile
0 500 1000 kms
0 400 800 mls

Did You Know? ▶

The Phoenicians were among the first explorers to leave the Mediterranean. They were skilled seamen, living in what is now Israel and Lebanon.

Carthage, in Tunisia, is ▶ now a ruin in the desert. When the Phoenicians founded it in 800 BC, it was a port in a fertile land.

landforms. Since they had no compasses, they sometimes got lost when clouds covered the stars and the Sun.

The Ancient Egyptians

In 2600 BC, the Egyptians made the first seagoing voyage ever recorded. Egypt was the greatest early civilization of the Mediterranean. In about 600 BC, the pharaoh of Egypt, Necho, started trading with Arabia and East Africa. This trade over land was slow. So Necho paid a Phoenician fleet to find a sea route around Africa. The Phoenicians did, but it took them three years — far too long to use as a trade route.

▲ A picture of one of the ancient world's greatest legendary explorers — Ulysses. The journey he took from Troy to Ithaca was described by the Greek poet Homer about 2,500 years ago.

Did You Know?

Hanno was a Phoenician from Carthage. In the fifth century BC, he left with 60 ships to start colonies on the west coast of Africa. On his trip, he saw "women with hairy bodies" — probably chimpanzees. "We caught three women, who bit and scratched," he wrote.

The Greeks

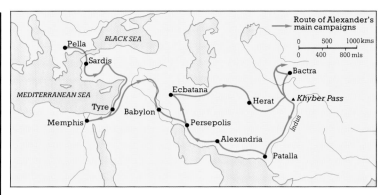

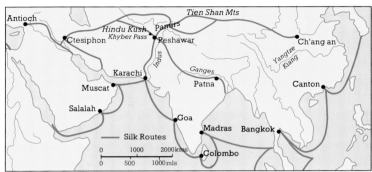

Upper: Alexander the ▼ Great led his conquering army along this route.

Lower: This map shows the ancient Silk Road and the spice routes across Asia. ▶

Alexander the Great, one of the world's greatest travelers. ▼

The Greeks were the greatest explorers of the ancient world. They set up over 100 colonies around the Mediterranean and the Black Sea. About 400 BC, the Greeks began to look beyond the Mediterranean area.

Alexander the Great

At age 23, Alexander was king of Macedonia — at that time, not part of Greece. In 334 BC, he led his army eastward to conquer Persia — now Iran — and India. He wanted to conquer the whole world, until he found out the world was much bigger than he thought. Alexander reached Afghanistan, marched through the Khyber Pass, and went down the Indus River. But he died of fever at the age of 33, in Babylon, near present-day Baghdad, Iraq.

Exploring the North

Very few Greeks headed north into the damp, cold lands of northern Europe. One of the first was Pytheas. He sailed to England and found out it was an island. He then went farther north to a land he called Thule. Today, we are not sure where Thule is, but it may have been in Norway or Iceland.

The Silk Road

The Chinese explored, too. The Chinese wanted to make links to the West so they could sell silk to the rich people of Europe. No one in Europe knew how to make silk. One Chinese explorer, Chang Chi'en, opened westward trading routes. Between 138 BC and 126 BC, Chang Chi'en explored the Tien Shan, Pamirs, and Hindu Kush as far west as the Khyber Pass. In 399 BC, a Buddhist monk, Fa Hsien, made a 15-year journey through India as far as Sri Lanka.

Part of the Silk Road in Kirghiz, in what is now the southern Soviet Union. ▼

9

3: | EXPANDING NATIONS

The Norsemen

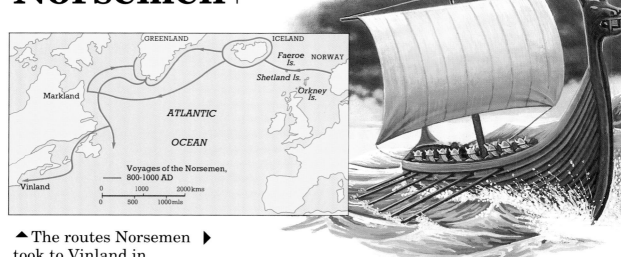

▲ The routes Norsemen ▶ took to Vinland in longships like the ones at right and below. ▼

Did You Know?

The Norsemen, expert sailors, used the wind, the Sun, birds, currents, water color, and ice and fog to navigate.

Before AD 1000, a brave new group of sailors, the Norsemen, explored the icy waters of the North Atlantic. They sailed in sturdy wooden ships called knorrs that held up to 30 people, with food and cattle.

East and West

The Norsemen ventured from their home in Scandinavia as far east as Constantinople, which they reached in AD 860. On the way, they went through Russia,

St. Brendan in his curragh

moving their ships over land from river to river. At about the same time, Norsemen traveled west to Iceland. One Icelander, Eric the Red, discovered Greenland in AD 982. Many Norsemen lived there until the climate became too cold.

Discovering Vinland

About AD 1000, Eric's son, Leif Ericsson, sailed farther west to a warmer, wooded area that he called Vinland. It was in North America. Leif had reached the New World 400 years before Christopher Columbus! But the native Indians living there attacked the Norsemen, forcing them to leave.

Saint Brendan, the Explorer-Saint

Saint Brendan may have been the first explorer to cross the Atlantic. After Christianity came to Ireland in AD 432, Irish monks traveled in open hide-covered boats, called curraghs, looking for islands so they could live simply. Brendan was one of these monks. A book over 1,400 years old tells how Brendan sailed west and found "crystal columns," which may have been icebergs, and "a globe of fire," which may have been a volcano. The book also describes beautiful islands to the west, perhaps the Bahamas. No one knows for sure if the story is really true. A modern explorer, Tim Severin, actually sailed across the Atlantic in a curragh.

◀ Norsemen often stayed home in the winter. In the summer, they traveled great distances to trade or explore.

Exploring the East

Arab Explorers

The Arabs were also curious about the world. They traveled by land or sea. Arabs visited the countries of Denmark, England, China, and Russia. The greatest Arabian traveler was young Ibn Batuta, from Morocco. In AD 1325, Ibn left on a journey that lasted nearly 30 years and covered over 75,000 miles (120,000 km)! He visited the holy cities of Mecca and Medina, then went on to explore the Middle East, Africa, India, Russia, and China. Ibn wrote books about his adventures. He described a roc, a mythical giant bird that could carry away humans!

The journeys of Ibn Batuta in the 1300s. ▶

Europeans and Asians traded goods for many centuries until the Mongols began attacking Europe and the Near East in the 1200s. Then Genghis Khan, their leader, died. Europeans could again travel eastward. The pope sent friars — holy men — east to make friends with the Mongols. An Italian friar, John Carpini, was the first European to travel 3,000 miles (4,800 km) to the Mongol capital, in 1245. He wrote about his long travels.

Marco Polo

Merchants soon followed the friars east. The most famous merchant traveler was Marco Polo. At age 17, he went east to China with his father and uncle. In 1275, the Polos arrived at the court of Kublai Khan. They were impressed by the khan's palace.

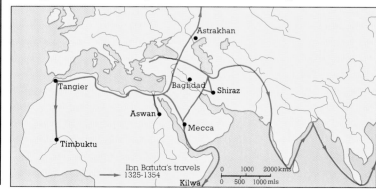

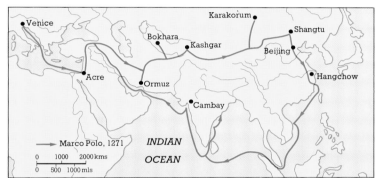

The Great Wall of China — built around 300 BC to keep out invaders.

◀ The routes of Marco Polo's 24 years of travel in China and other places in Asia.

The walls were gold and silver, and the dining hall could seat 6,000 people! Marco kept a diary of all the things he saw on his travels. He saw a city with 12,000 bridges, and he saw huge Chinese ships, called junks, that had 60 cabins. He returned home to Venice, Italy, 24 years after he left it. For the next 50 years, Europeans freely traveled to the east, until the Moslem nations would no longer allow them to pass through.

▲ The huge egg of the now extinct elephant bird (left) is much bigger than an ostrich egg (center) and the egg of a hummingbird (right). The mythical roc may have been based on the elephant bird.

Around Africa

This seventeenth-century map of Africa shows the correct coastline, but the interior was only a guess. ▶

▲Prince Henry the Navigator paid for many voyages but did not go on any himself.

Even though the Phoenicians had journeyed around Africa long before, most Europeans believed that Africa was a place of fire where rivers boiled.

Henry the Navigator

The Portuguese were the first Europeans to sail around Africa. Prince Henry the Navigator sent ships out to explore. One of them was the first European ship to cross the equator.

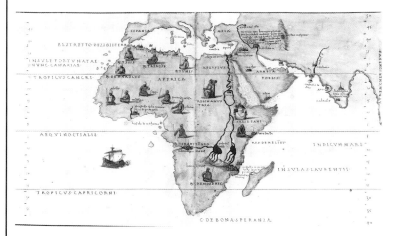

To India by Sea

Two Portuguese explorers sailed south to find a trade route to India. One was Pedro da Covihaol who landed on the coast of Ethiopia. Covilhao was surprised to find that many Africans had their own kind of

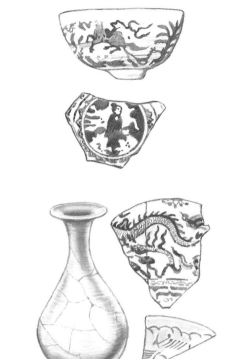

Christianity. The other was Bartholomew Dias, who reached the southern tip of Africa. The king named the tip the Cape of Good Hope because he hoped that sailors could now sail all the way to India. Finally, Vasco da Gama made the complete journey. During the two-year trip, 30 crew members died. But traders could now get valuable spices without crossing through enemy countries.

▼ Above left: British archaeologist Sir Mortimer Wheeler excavated at Kilwa, off the coast of Tanzania.

▲ Above: Chinese objects from Kilwa are from 600 to 800 years old. They show that early trade took place between China and Africa.

Palace ruins on Kilwa, an early trade center. ▼

Columbus and the New World

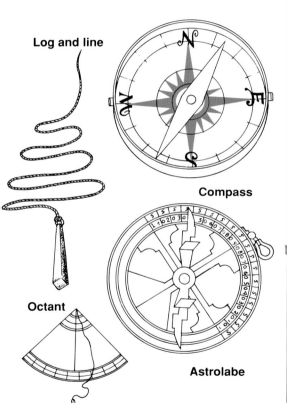

Log and line

Compass

Octant

Astrolabe

▲ Instruments used to navigate the seas.

A cross-section view of ▶ Columbus' first ship, the *Santa Maria*. The sailors were cramped in small spaces.

Christopher Columbus knew that the world was round. He thought that he could reach the East quicker by sailing across the Atlantic Ocean, instead of all the way around Africa. King Ferdinand and Queen Isabella of Spain thought such a journey might bring riches to Spain. They gave Columbus three ships and a hundred sailors for the voyage. In 1492, Columbus and his crew sailed westward into the unknown.

The Bahamas

After sailing for two months, the

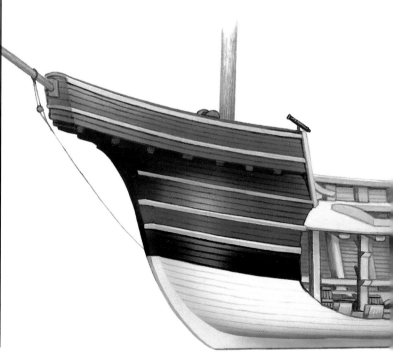

tired, hungry sailors decided to mutiny. Just then, the lookout sighted land! Soon, friendly people swam out to greet the ship. Columbus called these native people Indians because he thought he was near India. He was really in the Bahamas.

Columbus crossed the Atlantic three more times, bringing Spaniards to start a colony. Columbus never found the riches of the East that he was looking for. But he did find a whole new world.

▲After two months at sea, the sailors were cheered to see an island like this.

The Man Who Named a Continent

America took its name from an Italian called Amerigo Vespucci. His employers sent him to Spain to sell supplies to ships going to the New World. In Spain, he met Christopher Columbus. Vespucci later made voyages for Spain and for Portugal. He explored the coast of South America and was the first to describe it as a new continent, instead of as part of Asia. Martin Waldseemüller, a map-maker, suggested either "Amerige" or "America" as the continent's name. Later, people used the name for both continents.

Around the World

The route of Ferdinand Magellan and Juan del Cano, the captain who took over after Magellan died. ▶

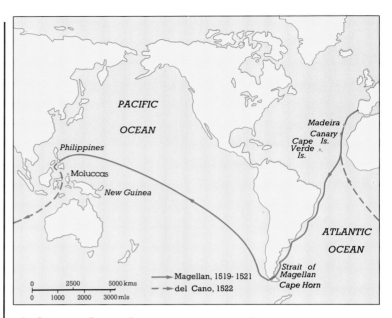

▲ This portrait shows Magellan as a calm, dreamy man. He was also a tough sea captain.

Right: A sixteenth-century ▶ Portuguese map that shows South America and the Strait of Magellan. Opposite: The strait in good weather — a shortcut to the Pacific. ▶ ▶

After the discovery of the New World, Ferdinand Magellan, a Portuguese employed by Spain, promised to find a route to the Far East. Magellan set sail in 1519 with five ships and a crew of 237. It was a long and hard voyage. One ship was wrecked early in a storm. Some of his men tried to mutiny. One ship

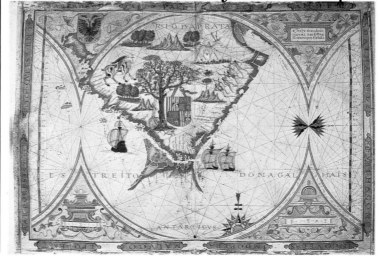

turned back in fear. Magellan faced icy storms and dangerous cliffs at the tip of South America. Luckily, he discovered a channel he could navigate through, now called the Strait of Magellan.

Into the Pacific

Food and water ran low as they crossed the huge Pacific Ocean. Twenty men died. The rest survived on rats, rotten biscuits, and leather. At last they reached the Philippines. Magellan and 40 of his men died in a battle they had joined to help a local chief. Two ships sailed on. The Portuguese captured one ship. The other finished the three-year voyage with 18 men, the first to sail around the world.

The Dragon Who Circled the World

The second great explorer to sail around the world was Sir Francis Drake, from England. Queen Elizabeth I hired him to raid Spanish galleons carrying gold and silver from Spanish America. In 1569, he glimpsed the Pacific Ocean beyond what is now Panama. He wanted to sail on it.

In 1577, Queen Elizabeth sent Drake around South America to the Asian islands for spices. If Drake could plunder a Spanish galleon or two on his way, so much the better.

When storms drove him off course, Drake found another way to pass around the tip of South America. Later, sailing across the Pacific, he captured one galleon carrying 20 tons of silver!

Looking for an easy way back to the Atlantic, he sailed as far north as Canada. He could not find a way east, so he sailed the rest of the way around the world to get home, bringing millions of dollars in Spanish treasure. The Spaniards called him the Dragon.

4: OPENING THE PACIFIC

The Southern Continent

This map of Australasia ▶ shows the routes of the Dutchman Abel Tasman and the Frenchman Louis de Bougainville.

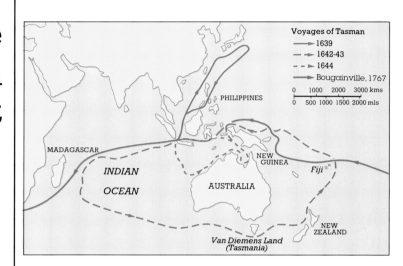

In the late sixteenth century, Europeans believed there was an undiscovered continent in the South Pacific. The Spaniards wanted to find it first. They even named the unseen place Australia, or "land of the south."

The Dutch

Willem Janszoon, a Dutch sailor, first sighted Australia, in 1606. In 1642, Abel Tasman, another Dutchman, became the first European to sail around Australia. He discovered New

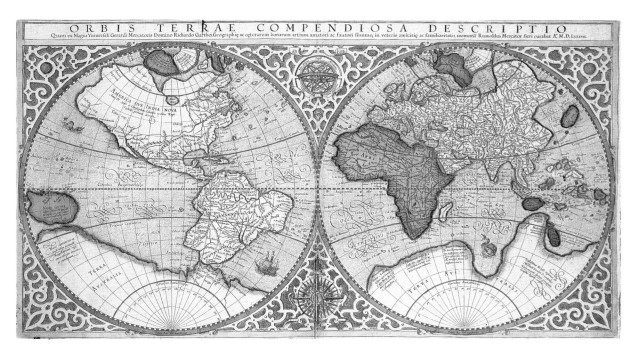

ORBIS TERRAE COMPENDIOSA DESCRIPTIO
Quam ex Magna Vniuersali Gerardi Mercatoris Domino Richardo Gartho, Geographiæ ac cæterarum bonarum artium amatori ac fautori summo, in veteris amicitiæ ac familiaritatis memoriâ Rumoldus Mercator fieri curabat A° M.D.LXXXVII.

Zealand, Tasmania, and some other South Pacific islands.

Louis de Bougainville

A French officer, Louis de Bougainville, took scientists along on a Pacific voyage in 1766-69. They made many discoveries, especially Jeanne Baré. This expert botanist was the first woman to take part in a great voyage of exploration.

▲ This 1595 map of the world shows a huge southern continent that no one had ever seen. The scientists of those days believed that the land was needed there to balance the northern continents.

◄ These Aboriginals were among the last to survive in Tasmania. Europeans, drink, and disease killed most of them in the 1860s.

21

Captain Cook

This map shows the three voyages of Captain Cook. ▶

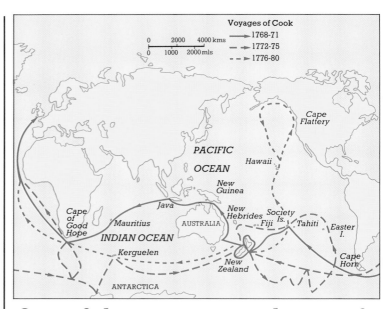

▲This portrait shows the humane and gentle side of Captain James Cook. He fed his men well to prevent diseases such as scurvy.

One of the greatest explorers of the Pacific Ocean was Captain James Cook of the British navy, born in 1728. Cook was an expert in mathematics and navigation, who was interested in charting the movements of planets. He also had a secret mission to find an undiscovered continent south of Australia.

Cook's Voyages

Cook made three voyages in the late 1700s. During his first voyage, he mapped several islands in the South Pacific, including New Zealand. On his second voyage, he sailed farther south. Although he did not reach Antarctica, he did find an icy

◀ Captain Cook's ship, the *Endeavour*, was a sturdy vessel that was over 97 feet (30 m) long.

region of fog and icebergs, where even his sails froze! On his third voyage, he discovered the Hawaiian Islands in 1778. He sailed north through the Bering Strait, searching for a sea route through North America. When ice and storms stopped him, he returned to Hawaii. There, in a fight over a stolen boat, some Hawaiians killed him.

The Man Who Found Longitude

An Englishman, John Harrison, invented a clock in 1761 that would keep accurate time at sea. For the first time, sailors could find their exact longitude — their ship's east or west position. They compared the local time with the time in England. By using Harrison's clock, Cook could navigate and map with great accuracy.

◀ On Cook's second visit to Hawaii, some local people stole one of his boats. When his men tried to get it back, a fight broke out and some Hawaiians killed Cook.

5: ACROSS THE NEW WORLD

The Northwest Passage

▲ Englishman Martin Frobisher was a strong man with a bad temper.

While the Spaniards were colonizing Central and South America, the British explored North America. They were convinced that they could find a sea passage through North America that connected the Atlantic and Pacific oceans. This route was known as the Northwest Passage.

Sir Martin Frobisher

In 1576, Martin Frobisher was one of the first people to look for the Northwest Passage. During his search, he and his men were surrounded by hostile Inuit in kayaks. When five of his men disappeared while exploring, Frobisher captured an Inuit and took him along to England. Frobisher made three trips in search of the Northwest Passage, but never found it.

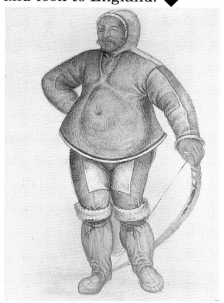

◀ Inuit attacked Frobisher's men as they explored Baffin Island.

The Inuit Frobisher captured and took to England. ▼

Polar bears present another danger for Arctic explorers. ▼

Henry Hudson

In 1610, Henry Hudson sailed to North America to find the Northwest Passage. When he reached Canada, Hudson spent the winter with his men in a huge bay, now called Hudson Bay. Later, his men mutinied. They set him adrift in an open boat, leaving him, his young son, and seven companions to die.

Moving Westward

The French explored interior North America, going by canoe and trading with the Indians. Jacques Cartier was the first Frenchman to explore Canada. He explored the Gulf of St. Lawrence in 1534 and the St. Lawrence River the next year.

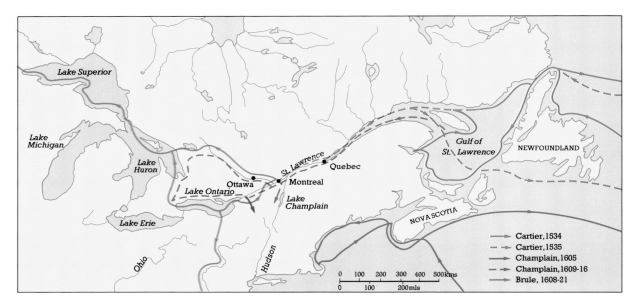

	Cartier, 1534
	Cartier, 1535
	Champlain, 1605
	Champlain, 1609-16
	Brule, 1608-21

▲ This map shows the routes of the early French explorers in North America.

Later Explorers

Sixty years later, Samuel de Champlain looked for a way across the continent. He explored around Lake Ontario and founded a colony in that area. At about the same time, Etienne Brulé explored Lake Ontario, Lake Huron, and Lake Superior, nearly reaching the center of the continent. Other

Frenchmen went south and west to the Mississippi River. In 1682, Robert Cavelier de La Salle explored the Mississippi all the way to the Gulf of Mexico. Alexander Mackenzie explored the great Mackenzie River. He also explored westward from Lake Athabasca, becoming the first European to reach the Pacific Ocean overland, in 1793.

▲ Early European explorers and settlers traded with the Indians. In exchange for guns and metal tools, the Indians gave them furs that were highly valued in Europe.

Watched by Indians, Jacques Cartier's 1535 expedition sails westward up the St. Lawrence River. ▼

Expansion from the East

Frontiersmen lived ▶
dangerous lives. They
traveled over unknown
territory and risked being
attacked by both Indians
and bears.

This is the basic outfit
every frontiersman needed
in the wilderness. ▼

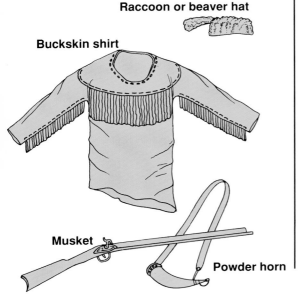

Raccoon or beaver hat

Buckskin shirt

Musket

Powder horn

By the mid-1700s, the east coast settlements were crowded. So people began moving westward.

Daniel Boone

For a hundred years, men had been crossing the Appalachian Mountains to hunt. The best-known frontiersman was Daniel

Boone. He hunted and explored in Kentucky for years. Settlers began following after him.

Lewis and Clark

In 1803, the US bought from

◀ Wagon trains rolled along trails that were pioneered by the first explorers of the West. This wagon train heads across the prairies into the Rocky Mountains.

France a vast tract of territory that needed to be explored. The leaders of the expedition were Meriwether Lewis and William Clark. They set out in 1804 across the midwestern prairies. Soon they were in unknown land, facing the Rocky Mountains, which looked too high to cross. Luckily, one expedition member was married to a Shoshone woman, Sacajawea. She guided them through the mountains, and later saved their lives from hostile tribes. Lewis and Clark and their companions went down the Columbia River to the Pacific. They returned safely the next year with valuable notes and maps. They had covered 7,500 miles (12,000 km) in 28 months.

A frontiersman from the time of Daniel Boone — between 1750 and 1800. ▼

6: THE WILDS OF ASIA

Across Siberia

▲ A painting of Peter the Great. He sent out expeditions to explore the northeastern territories of the Russian Empire.

Until the 1550s, Siberia was unexplored. In 1581, 1,600 Cossacks marched over the Ural Mountains to begin the Russian Empire's conquest of northern Asia. By 1640, the Russians had crossed Asia to the Pacific coast.

Peter the Great
Peter the Great (1672-1725), the tsar of Russia, sent explorers to far eastern Siberia. The most outstanding explorer of this area was Vitus Bering. He sailed north through the gap 40 miles (64 km) wide between Asia and North America. In 1741, he

This map shows the ▶ routes Vitus Bering took in exploring the coasts of Siberia and Alaska.

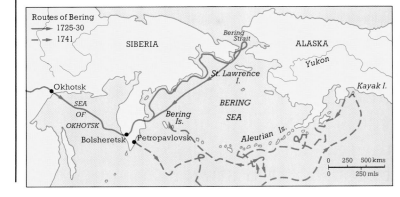

explored the coast of Alaska. He was shipwrecked on barren Bering Island. He and 28 of his men died there of scurvy.

Exploring the Tien Shan

The greatest Russian traveler, Nikolai Przhevalski, explored the rugged, unmapped Tien Shan mountains of central Asia in the 1870s. There, Przhevalski discovered the only known wild horse. It is named after him.

▲ The Tien Shan range forms a vast barrier between the Soviet Union and China.

▲ Przhevalski's woolly horse can live in icy central Asian winters.

31

The Himalayas

▲ Rock climbing and mountain climbing became popular sports in the nineteenth century.

The Potala, a great ▶ monastery, overlooks Lhasa. This city in Tibet was once called the Forbidden City because foreigners were not permitted there.

After the Polos, few Westerners traveled over the Himalayas to China. A Spaniard, Benedict de Goes, went there in 1603-05 to find out if Cathay and China were the same place. In 1661, two Jesuit missionaries, Albert d'Orville and John Grueber, went

◀ At 29,028 feet (8,848 m) high, the triangular peak of Everest is the highest in the world (left). But it is almost equaled by other Himalayan giants, like Nuptse (center) and Lhotse (right).

to China to set up a trade route. They were the first Europeans to see Lhasa, the capital of Tibet.

Mapmaking

Travelers usually took regular routes through the Himalayas. But mapmakers had to go off these paths. George Everest was the greatest mapmaker. Mt. Everest, the world's highest mountain, is named after him. Perhaps the greatest explorer of central Asia was Sven Hedin. He made many journeys and maps of the region. On one trip, between 1894-97, Hedin traveled 12,000 miles (19,000 km) and made 552 pages of maps. Other mapmakers were native scholars from India, called Pundits. They explored remote areas, often in the disguise of pilgrims.

Did You Know?
In 1953, Sir Edmund Hillary and Tenzing Norgay became the first people to reach the top of Mount Everest.

▲ Sven Hedin, a Swedish explorer, spent most of his life traveling in China and India. He was 70 years old when this picture was taken.

The Sands of Arabia

Mecca — the city where ▶
Muhammad, the founder
of Islam, was born — is
the holiest city in the
Moslem world. At the
center is the Kaaba, a
square building that
Islamic scripture says
Abraham built. Mecca is
closed to non-Moslems.

The Arabs knew their own world beyond the Red Sea. But the Europeans did not. They had to find out about it by sending out expeditions to explore it.

Mecca

Two things kept explorers out of the holy city of Mecca — the harsh desert and non-Moslems being forbidden there. An Italian, Ludovico di Varthema, the first European to see Mecca, visited it with some pilgrims in about 1500. Danish scientists made the first official exploration

of Arabia in 1762. Unluckily, all but one died of disease. Johann Burckhardt was more successful. He learned Arabic, dressed like an Arab, and then traveled up the Nile. In 1813, he was the first European to see the great rock temple of Abu Simbel, with its statues 60 feet (18 m) tall. The Arabs so respected Burkhardt that they declared him a Moslem and allowed him to visit Mecca. Richard Burton visited Mecca, disguised as an Afghan doctor. During World War I, the Arabs rose up against Turkish rule. T. E. Lawrence — Lawrence of Arabia — fought for them, and explored the Arabian desert. Later, he wrote about his experiences.

▲ Top: The Empty Quarter of southern Arabia is the world's largest sand desert.

▲ Above: Wilfred Thesiger was the last European to cross the Empty Quarter, in 1948-50. The first was Bertram Thomas, in 1930-31.

7: SOUTH AMERICA

The Search for El Dorado

In 1533, the Spaniards conquered the Inca in South America. They were interested only in taking as much gold as they could find.

The Gilded Man

The Spaniards heard about a tribe in Colombia that had an unusual ceremony. Every year, the people covered their chief with gold dust that he later washed off. The Spaniards called this chief El Dorado, "the gilded man." Actually, the tribe was small and had little gold.

Inset: The route of the Orellana expedition down the Amazon. Below: The Amazon runs through the largest rain forest in the world. ▼

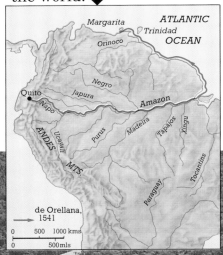

ATLANTIC OCEAN
Margarita
Trinidad
Orinoco
Negro
Quito
Napo
Japura
Amazon
ANDES MTS.
Ucayali
Purus
Madeira
Tapajos
Xingu
Paraguay
Tocantins

de Orellana, 1541
0   500   1000 kms
0   500 mls

Exploring the Amazon

The Spaniards wanted to find El Dorado. Gonzalo Pizarro and Francisco de Orellana marched 70 men down from the Andes into the tropical rain forest of the Amazon basin. After a month, they could find no food except frogs and snakes. They built a boat, and Orellana took 50 men to search for food. When the swift current swept them down the Amazon River, Pizarro and the rest turned back. Orellana and his men had to fight many hostile tribes before they reached the Atlantic, a journey of over 3,000 miles (5,000 km). They were the first Europeans to cross South America.

▲ The Inca used gold only for ornaments, not for money. This is a gold death mask made in Peru around AD 1200.

Lake Guatavita, in present-day Colombia, where the chief, known as El Dorado, washed gold dust from his body. Orellana and his men never found the tribe. ▼

Into the Amazon

The Humboldt Current sweeps north from the Antarctic, cooling the coast of South America. ▼

Chimborazo, a snow-capped volcano in the Andes. Alexander von Humboldt was the first to climb it, in 1802. He reached a height of 19,286 feet (5,878 m), setting a record for 30 years. ▶

The Amazon basin explorers were mostly scientists. The first, Frenchman Charles-Marie de la Condamine, examined the area in 1743. He found a great deal of plant and animal study to be done in the Amazon region.

Alexander von Humboldt

The greatest scientist-explorer was a German, Alexander von Humboldt. In 1799, he and French botanist Aimé Bonpland followed the Orinoco River. They discovered many strange creatures — piranhas, stingrays, electric eels, and freshwater dolphins. They also saw the Casiquiare Canal, a natural waterway that connects the Orinoco to the Amazon. Later, in the Andes, they climbed the

volcano Chimborazo, 20,577 feet (6,272 m) high. Humboldt got up to about 1,300 feet (400 m) from the top, but altitude sickness and an uncrossable ravine forced him to turn back.

The Humboldt Current

Humboldt discovered the cause of the desert in Peru. Although it is near the equator, the ocean is kept cold by a current from Antarctica. This is the Humboldt Current, and its cold keeps the area too dry for rain to fall.

▲ The explorer-scientist Humboldt (standing) at a camp high in the Andes.

A portrait of Alexander von Humboldt. ▼

SOUTH AMERICA

The Naturalists

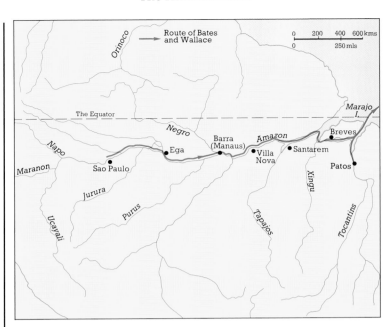

▲ A flock of protesting birds attacks Henry Bates as he captures a toucan for his collection.

In 1848, Henry Bates and Alfred Wallace, two English scientists, studied Amazon life to learn how different species started.

Collecting Species

In several years, Bates collected about 14,000 species of insects, over half of them new. But Wallace lost his collection in a shipboard fire. Hamilton Rice, from the US, tried to find the source of the Orinoco River, but hostile tribes drove him away. A Brazilian, Candido Rondon, made many trips to meet Indian tribes. He once traveled with former US president Theodore Roosevelt.

Roosevelt said the Amazon rain forest was a "green hell."

Mapping the Amazon
The best-known explorer of the Amazon was Percy Fawcett. For years there, he had mapped unexplored areas. In 1925, he and his son went to search for an ancient lost city. They vanished without a trace. Indians may have killed them.

▲ Wildlife of the Amazon.

Colonel Percy Fawcett. He and his son disappeared in the Amazon rain forest in 1925. ▼

Across the Sahara

Timbuktu

In 1824, Major Alexander Laing of the British army set out to find Timbuktu. It took him over a year, and Tuareg tribesmen nearly killed him. Laing was the first European to cross the Sahara Desert from north to south and enter Timbuktu. He never lived to describe this famous city. His guide killed him soon after he left it. René Caillié, a Frenchman, was the first European to describe Timbuktu. He reached the city in 1828.

At the end of the 1700s, the interior of Africa was still unknown to Europeans. British explorers decided to go there in search of wealth, scientific information, and new lands to colonize. The first goal was to locate Timbuktu, visited 400 years earlier by Ibn Batuta. Another goal was to find the source of the Niger River.

North African desert traders. ▶

Mungo Park mapped the Niger River. ▼

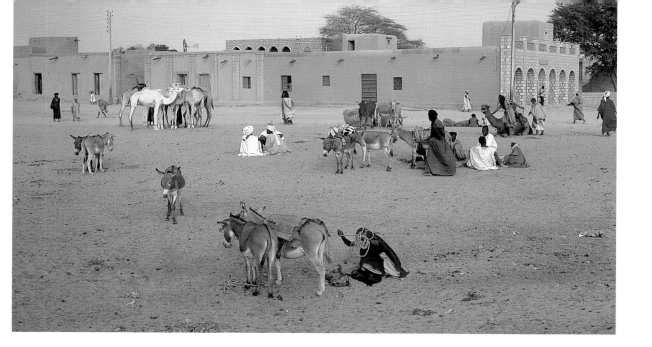

The Niger River

In 1795, Mungo Park, a Scottish doctor, set out to map the Niger River. He explored it for 300 miles (480 km) downstream. In 1805, he returned with 40 Europeans to find its mouth. They set out from the Gambia River, but few lived to reach the Niger. The rest, including Park, died before reaching the mouth. In 1822, three men traveled to Africa's Lake Chad, which some thought was the source of the Niger River. They were the first Europeans to see the lake. One man died, but Hugh Clapperton and Dixon Denham returned with amazing reports of African kingdoms south of the Sahara.

▲ Timbuktu, once a wealthy city, sits on the southern edge of the Sahara Desert.

Tuareg tribesmen like this man and the Arabs have traded in Timbuktu for centuries. ▼

The Source of the Nile

This map shows three ▶ expeditions to find the source of the Nile.

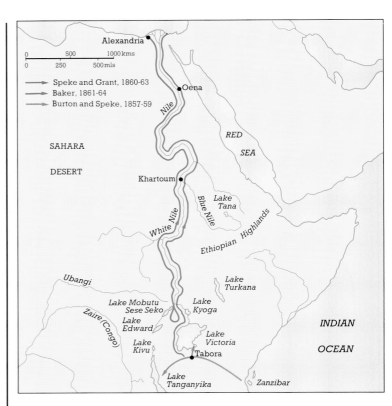

▲ Richard Burton once disguised himself as an Afghan so he could enter Mecca, the holy Moslem city forbidden to non-Moslems.

By the middle of the 1800s, the source of the Nile River was not yet known. Ptolemy, the Greek geographer, said it rose between "the Mountains of the Moon." The British Royal Geographical Society sent an expedition in 1856 to discover the source of the Nile. The leader was Richard Burton, an army officer who learned 25 different languages.

Lake Victoria

Burton and his companion, John Hanning Speke, discovered Lake Tanganyika in 1857. Both men

became sick, but Speke was able to go on. He traveled north to find a great lake, Lake Victoria. Speke was sure this was the Nile's source. He returned before Burton and broke the news. Speke soon organized another expedition, and James Grant joined him. They found where one branch of the Nile flows out of Lake Victoria. On the way back, they met Samuel Baker and his wife, also searching for the Nile's source. The Bakers found Murchison Falls and Lake Albert in 1864.

▲Murchison Falls, where the Nile River thunders out of Lake Albert.

Mount Kilimanjaro, in Tanzania. Up until the nineteenth century, people believed that the source of the Nile lay somewhere near here. ▼

Missionary Explorers

The exploration routes of ▶
David Livingstone and
Henry Morton Stanley
through central Africa.

Livingstone explored the
Zambezi River in 1855-56.
He reported that it was
calm. At that time he did
not know of the impassable
Quebrabasa rapids. ▼

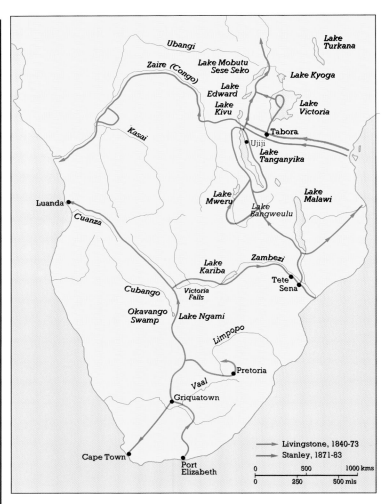

Livingstone, 1840-73
Stanley, 1871-83

David Livingstone is a famous
name among explorers. In 1841,
he went to southern Africa as a
missionary. He was among the
first to cross the Kalahari Desert.
He found Lake Ngami. Next, he
crossed Africa from coast to
coast, searching for a good trade
route. In 1858, he led a British
expedition up the Zambezi River,
but impassable rapids blocked
his way. Later, in 1866, he began

searching for the sources of the Nile and Congo rivers. He ran out of money and supplies and fell ill in Ujiji, on the shore of Lake Tanganyika. The world thought he was lost or dead.

Henry Morton Stanley

Just then, Henry Morton Stanley, a US news reporter, arrived with supplies. Stanley spoke those famous words, "Dr. Livingstone, I presume?" When Livingstone got well, he went on searching. He died in 1873, still exploring. Stanley himself led several more expeditions. He completed the exploration of central Africa by traveling the entire length of the Congo River.

The boat Livingstone used for sailing up the Zambezi River. His way was blocked by the impassable rapids he missed finding earlier. ▼

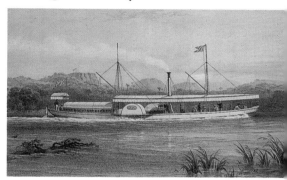

On a later expedition, Livingstone fell ill. His food and medicine had been stolen. Stanley (left) arrived with fresh supplies just in time. ▼

9: AUSTRALIA'S INTERIOR

Across the Great Range

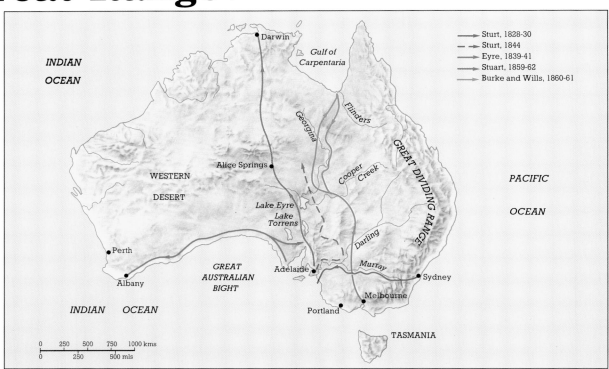

Sturt, 1828-30
Sturt, 1844
Eyre, 1839-41
Stuart, 1859-62
Burke and Wills, 1860-61

INDIAN OCEAN

Darwin

Gulf of Carpentaria

Flinders

Georgina

Alice Springs

Cooper Creek

GREAT DIVIDING RANGE

PACIFIC OCEAN

WESTERN

DESERT

Lake Eyre
Lake Torrens

Darling

Murray

Adelaide

Sydney

Perth

GREAT AUSTRALIAN BIGHT

Melbourne

Albany

Portland

INDIAN OCEAN

TASMANIA

0   250   500   750   1000 kms
0   250   500 mls

▲ The routes of the main expeditions of Australia's outback, or interior.

For decades after the British first settled in Australia, few crossed the Great Dividing Range along the eastern shore. Only the Aboriginals lived in the outback, as Australia's interior is called.

Mapping the Interior
In 1829, Charles Sturt took six others and explored down the

Murrumbidgee and Murray rivers to the southern coast. They then rowed back against the current for nearly 1,000 miles (1,600 km). But their reports of good land started colonists moving west. About ten years later, Edward Eyre left Adelaide to explore northward.

▲ The Darling River and others like it helped explorers reach Australia's interior.

◀ Cliffs like these in the Great Dividing Range, 500 feet (150 m) high, were a major barrier to explorers.

Edward Eyre and Wylie survived the 1840 exploration of Australia's southern coast. ▼

When deserts stopped him, he turned west instead. He explored 1,000 miles (1,600 km) of the southern desert coast, which did not have a single river. Two guides killed his companion and stole the supplies. Eyre and one faithful Aboriginal, Wylie, got food from a French ship. More weeks of travel brought them to Albany, near the west coast.

AUSTRALIA'S INTERIOR

The Simpson Desert

Charles Sturt starting off on his journey of 1844. He hoped to find a great inland sea, but found only seas of grass, sand, and rock.

Robert Burke was brave, but his bad temper made him unpopular. ▼

In 1844, Charles Sturt led an expedition to find an inland sea that he believed existed in the interior. The men spent months in desert heat up to 132°F (55°C). Then they entered the Simpson Desert, a wasteland of rock and sand about as large as South Carolina or New Brunswick. Discouraged, Sturt turned back.

The Telegraph Race
In 1859, when the Australian government decided to link north and south by telegraph, it offered a huge sum of money to the first person who could make the crossing. Two rival groups set out in 1860. John Stuart's group reached farther north than any European had

gone before. But when he was about 300 miles (500 km) from the northern coast, he ran out of food and had to turn back. Two years later, he made it all the way. Robert Burke, the first to use camels, led the second team. He split his men into two groups, one to wait for supplies to arrive, the other to hurry north. Burke and William Wills then rushed to the coast, the first Europeans to cross Australia south to north. The men had all planned to meet at Cooper Creek, but they could not find each other again. All died of starvation except John King. He was found wandering in the desert with Aboriginals.

▲ Cooper Creek was the meeting place for Burke and his men. Most of them died in the deserts near here.

Here is a camel caravan like the one Burke used for his expedition. He was the first to bring these animals into Australia. Camels travel better in deserts than horses. ▼

The North Pole

This map shows the routes of the major expeditions in the Arctic. ▶

First to the Pole

Robert Peary of the US claimed to be the first person to reach the North Pole, in 1909.

An Inuit family, adapted to the severe cold of the far north. ▼

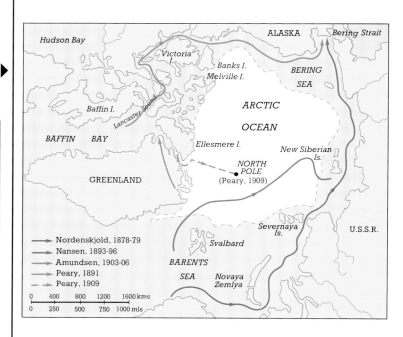

Hudson Bay · ALASKA · Bering Strait · Victoria I. · Banks I. · Melville I. · BERING SEA · Baffin I. · Lancaster Sound · ARCTIC OCEAN · BAFFIN BAY · Ellesmere I. · New Siberian Is. · NORTH POLE (Peary, 1909) · GREENLAND · Severnaya Is. · U.S.S.R. · Svalbard · BARENTS SEA · Novaya Zemlya

→ Nordenskjold, 1878-79
→ Nansen, 1893-96
→ Amundsen, 1903-06
→ Peary, 1891
- - → Peary, 1909

0 400 800 1200 1600 kms
0 250 500 750 1000 mls

In the nineteenth century, several British explorers unsuccessfully tried to find the Northwest Passage north of Canada that would connect the Pacific and Atlantic oceans.

Discovering Magnetic North

In 1829, John Ross led the Arctic expedition that discovered the north magnetic pole. He spent three years in the Arctic before

Nansen's Way

A Norwegian, Fridtjof Nansen, came up with a new way to reach the North Pole. He designed a ship's hull, shaped to slip up out of the water when ice closed in. After sailing north, Nansen let his ship, the *Fram*, freeze in. He went on with sleds and kayaks. Nansen came within 240 miles (386 km) of the pole.

crushing ice forced him and his crew to abandon ship. The men lived in a small makeshift house during the Arctic winter. Luckily, a whaling ship rescued them. In 1845, Sir John Franklin led a less fortunate expedition. He and many others died of disease after his ship became frozen in ice. Some of the men tried to walk on the ice toward safety, but they died on the way. Baron Nils Nordenskjöld, a Swedish explorer, was the first to sail the Northeast Passage, which runs north of Siberia, in 1878-79. And the Northwest Passage was finally navigated in 1903-06 by Roald Amundsen, the Norwegian polar explorer.

Fridtjof Nansen was both a scientist and an explorer. He was an oceanographer and a zoologist. He was also a skilled artist. ▼

The South Pole

The main routes in search ▶
of the South Pole.

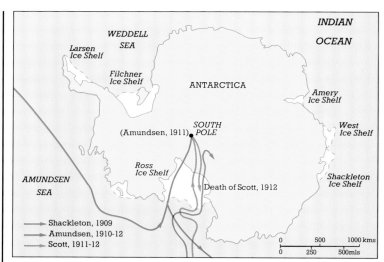

▲ Robert Falcon Scott
writes in his diary at his
camp before setting out for
the South Pole.

Camping is dangerous in ▶
the Antarctic, where high
winds whip the snow into
a foglike, blinding whiteout,
and bare flesh can freeze
in a minute.

Antarctica was the last continent
to be explored. Many explorers
tried to be the first to reach the
South Pole.

The Race to the South Pole
Ernest Shackleton, a British
explorer, set out for the South
Pole in 1908. He discovered the
Beardmore Glacier. He ran short

of food 100 miles (160 km) from the pole and had to turn back. In 1911, two men raced for the pole. Roald Amundsen, from Norway, used Arctic furs and sledge dogs. British expedition leader Robert Scott had ponies and motorized sledges. The sledges soon broke down. The ponies starved and froze and had to be shot. For four weeks, Scott and his men hauled their supplies on foot. Then Scott and four men hurried the last 178 miles (286 km) to the pole — only to find that Amundsen had been there 34 days earlier, on December 14, 1911. He had made the trip in seven weeks of dog sledging. Scott and his four men died on the return journey.

▲ The Beardmore Glacier — the best route to the South Pole for early explorers.

Here is Shackleton's well-stocked base hut. ▼

The Bitter End

From the South Pole, Scott and his men started back to their base camp, 800 miles (1,300 km) away. They began to die of starvation and exhaustion. One died on the Beardmore Glacier. Another man wandered away. The other three died 12 days later, only 11 miles (18 km) from a food cache. Scott's last diary entry asked the world to care for their families.

◀ Roald Amundsen raises the Norwegian flag over the South Pole.

The Last Unknown

Ernest Shackleton and his ship, the *Endurance*. The vessel was locked in ice for eight months, and then it sank. ▶

The type of clothing modern explorers need to survive in the Arctic or Antarctic. ▼

Knit headgear

Padded jacket with hood

Padded overpants

Lined gloves

Snow boots

Ernest Shackleton made one of Antarctica's most heroic journeys. He went there in 1915. His ship froze in the ice and later sank. He and his 28 crewmen camped for four months on the ice until it broke up. They rowed to a small island. Then Shackleton and five men sailed in a small boat for 870 miles (1,400 km) to reach an island whaling station for help. All of his men were saved.

Mapping and Photographing

Today, our interest in Antarctica

is scientific. In 1946, the US sent a crew to map and photograph over half the coast. In 1957, a British team crossed Antarctica in snowmobiles. They found that the ice cap averages 1.5 miles (2.5 km) thick. It holds as much water as the Atlantic Ocean!

The 12-Nation Treaty

In 1959, 12 nations signed a treaty, promising not to claim any more land in Antarctica and to use the area only for peaceful scientific research.

▲ Icebreakers like this make modern Antarctic research safer.

Frontiers of the Future

Today, it is easier and safer to explore our world. Now satellites can photograph the Earth from unlimited heights, and submersibles can reach the deepest ocean floors.

New Challenges

Many challenges still remain for curious and brave explorers. For example, the deepest known cave is in France. It goes down 3,872 feet (1,180 m). Mammoth Cave, in Kentucky, is the longest cave, stretching 186 miles (300 km).

▲ Scientists exploring the mysteries of the world's ocean depths. This submersible craft can withstand the great pressure of water near the ocean floor.

Space exploration is the ▶ next great challenge for humans. Scientists are shown gathering rock samples on the Moon.

Miles of caves wait to be explored. There are also many discoveries to be made in the tropical rain forests. The Amazon shelters little-known tribes, animals not yet recorded, and plants that may have properties valuable to humans. Space exploration is expensive and risky. A single mistake can destroy a mission. But the knowledge gained is worth the risk for the astronauts, who in the future will travel into this great unknown frontier.

▲ Mountain climber Chris Bonington in the Himalayas, using a computer to record his notes.

This man is spelunking in the Pyrenees, in France. Cave exploring, or spelunking, is exciting, but dangerous. ▼

Glossary

Amazon basin: The large area in South America from which all the water and excess rainfall runs into the Amazon River and the smaller rivers that flow into the Amazon.

Botanist: A scientist who studies plants.

Civilization: A stage of development reached by a nation or a group of nations with a complex social order, written language, and advances in art, science, and government.

Compass: An instrument that contains a movable magnetic needle that always points to magnetic north. It is used in finding direction. The Chinese invented the compass.

Cossacks: People who originally came from southeastern Russia, known for their expert horsemanship and fighting abilities.

Curragh: An Irish word, meaning a small boat used for rowing. It is made by stretching skins or tarred canvas over a wooden frame.

Equator: An imaginary circle around Earth, lying halfway between the North and South poles.

Expedition: A journey that is usually well organized and has a purpose — for example, military or scientific.

Frontiersman: Any person among the first to enter new territory west of the American frontier. These men were fur trappers, hunters, and traders with the Indians. They opened new trails in the wilderness that were later followed by settlers.

Galleon: A large Spanish sailing ship of the fifteenth and sixteenth centuries that had three or four decks at the stern, or rear end, of the vessel. It was used as both a warship and for trading.

Ice age: A period in Earth's history when the climate was extremely cold and glaciers spread over much of the land. There were many ice ages; the most recent one ended about 11,000 years ago.

Inuit: A member of the people native to Alaska, northern Canada, Greenland, and eastern Siberia, once known as Eskimos.

Jesuit: A member of the Society of Jesus, a Roman Catholic religious order.

Junk: A flat-bottomed Chinese sailing ship, with battens stiffening the sails, and a high poop deck.

Kayak: A type of canoe enclosed by a deck with a snugly fitting hole in it for the paddler. Kayaks were first used by the Inuit of North America and Greenland.

Longitude: An east or west position on the globe. Lines of longitude are imaginary lines on the Earth that run from the North Pole to the South Pole.

Mecca: A city in Saudi Arabia, where Muhammad, the founder of Islam, was born. It is a holy place and center of pilgrimage for Moslems.

Merchant: Someone who lives by buying and selling products. This is usually done on a large scale and often includes trading with foreign peoples and countries.

Missionary: Someone who actively tries to convert people to his or her religion. Missionaries often travel to foreign countries for this purpose.

Moslem: A follower of the faith of Islam, founded by the Prophet Mohammed.

Mutiny: A revolt against authority. This word is used most often for a revolt in the military or on board ship.

Navigate: To lay out a course for a ship to sail, often using the stars and special instruments.

North magnetic pole: The place toward which a compass needle points. It is not located exactly at the North Pole itself.

Oceanographer: A person who studies the ocean environment, including the waters, bottoms, depths, animals, plants, and so on.

Outback: The thinly settled, flat, dry inland region of Australia.

Pilgrim: A person who travels to holy places in order to worship.

Przhevalski's horse: The last surviving wild horse of prehistoric times, now existing mostly in zoos. Early Stone Age people painted this horse on cave walls in France and Spain, and carved its likeness in stone, horn, and bone. Nikolai Przhevalski discovered this horse in the Altai Mountains of Mongolia in the 1870s.

Roc: An extremely large bird that legends speak of, but which does not really exist.

Sacajawea: A Shoshone woman, born around 1788, who died in 1884. She lived among the Plains

Indians as a captive, but later married a French-Canadian trapper. When he joined the Lewis and Clark Expedition, she and her baby went with him. She acted as a guide and interpreter, and later stayed behind among the Shoshone of Wyoming's Wind River.

Satellite: Something that rotates around a larger object. This might be something natural — like the Moon orbiting Earth — or artificial, like Sputnik or Landsat.

Scripture: The sacred writings of any religion.

Scurvy: A disease caused by a lack of vitamin C, which is found in fresh fruit and vegetables. People on long sea voyages were once vulnerable to this disease because their diet did not contain these foods.

Shoshone: A North American Indian tribe living in scattered groups in parts of the northern Rocky Mountain states. Most were hunter-gatherers, but those in Wyoming and Montana lived the same way as the Plains Indians, with feather headdresses, tepees, and horses.

Silk: A fine thread spun by the silkworm — the larva of a certain type of moth — when it builds its cocoon. People use the thread to make beautiful and expensive fabrics.

Sled: A vehicle that moves on runners over snow and ice. A larger sled is called a sledge.

Species: A group of plants, animals, or other life forms whose members are similar to each other and can breed together.

Spelunking: The exploring and studying of caves.

Submersible: A vehicle that can operate under water at great depths. Scientists and marine biologists use submersibles to study life in the oceans and seas.

Telegraph: A device for sending messages using coded electric signals sent through wires.

Toucan: A large bird found in Central America and tropical South America. It has a large bill of several colors, which may be longer than the bird's body length of one to two feet (30-61 cm). Toucans nest in tree hollows, and most of them live on fruit.

Tropics: Two imaginary parallel lines around Earth, running east-west. One, the Tropic of Cancer, is north of the equator. The other, the Tropic of Capricorn, is south of it. Between these lines lies the tropical zone, or the tropics, an area of great heat and humidity.

Whiteout: A visual condition in polar regions that makes the snow-covered ground and the white sky appear as one even shade of white. During a whiteout, people cannot see any shadows, clouds, or the horizon, and they cannot tell distance or direction.

Zoologist: A person who studies animals and the animal kingdom.

Index